MYSTERY TRAIN

Books by David Wojahn

Glassworks (1987)
Icehouse Lights (1982)

DAVID WOJAHN

-\/\/\-\/\/\-\/\/\-

MYSTERY TRAIN

UNIVERSITY OF PITTSBURGH PRESS

Published by the University of Pittsburgh Press, Pittsburgh, Pa. 15260
Copyright © 1990, David Wojahn
Baker & Taylor International, London
Manufactured in the United States of America

Library of Congress Cataloging-in-Publication Data
Wojahn, David, 1953–
    Mystery train / David Wojahn.
        p.   cm. —'(Pitt poetry series)
    Includes bibliographical references.
    ISBN 0-8229-3637-2.— ISBN 0-8229-5429-X (pbk.)
    I. Title. II. Series.
PS3573.044M9   1990
811'.54—dc20   89-39343
                                                                    CIP

Acknowledgment is made to the following publications in which some of these poems appeared, often in earlier versions: *Boulevard* ("C Train Home: Lou Reed After the Wake of Delmore Schwartz, July 1966," "Delmore Schwartz at the First Performance of the Velvet Underground: New York, 1966," "Francis Ford Coppola and Anthropologist Interpreter Teaching Gartewienna Tribesmen to Sing 'Light My Fire,' Philippine Jungle, 1978," "John Berryman Listening to Robert Johnson's 'King of the Delta Blues,' January 1972," "Necromancy: The Last Days of Brian Jones, 1968," and "W.C.W. Watching Presley's Second Appearance on 'The Ed Sullivan Show,' Mercy Hospital, Newark, 1956"); *Denver Quarterly* ("Armageddon: Private Gabriel Calvin Wojahn, 1900–18" and "Futures"); *The Gettysburg Review* ("The Resurrection of the Dead: Port Glasgow, 1950"); *Iowa Review* (" 'Mystery Train': Janis Joplin Leaves Port Arthur for Points West, 1964" and "Photographer at Altamont: The Morning After, 1968"); *Ironwood* ("No Gesture: Ceremony"); *The Kenyon Review* (" 'It's Only Rock and Roll But I Like It': The Fall of Saigon, 1975" and "Matins: James Brown and His Famous Flames Tour the South, 1958"); *New England Review and Bread Loaf Quarterly* ("Shroud"); *The North American Review* ("Diary Pages: Amsterdam"); *Ploughshares* ("Double Exposures" and "The Recent Work"); *Poetry* ("A Fifteenth Anniversary: John Berryman"); *Poetry East* ("Signs and Wonders"); *Prairie Schooner* ("Garry Owen" and "In Hiding"); *Seneca Review* ("Students"); *Shankpainter* ("Pharaoh's Palace"); *Sonora Review* ("For Charles Bovary"); and *The Yale Review* ("Azimuth" and "Posthumous Life").

Several of these poems also appeared in a limited edition, *Rilke's Children,* The Larkspur Press, 1987. I would also like to thank the Indiana Commission for the Arts for a writing fellowship and, especially, the trustees of the estate of Amy Lowell for an Amy Lowell Traveling Poetry Scholarship. Thanks are also due to the Centrum Foundation of Port Townsend, Washington, and to the Corporation of Yaddo for hospitality during the beginning and the completion of this collection.

The publication of this book is supported by grants
from the National Endowment for the Arts
in Washington, D.C., a Federal agency,
and the Pennsylvania Council on the Arts.

Again, for Lynda

Contents

Contents

Contents

For the wild thorns grow tame
And will do nothing to oppose the flame . . .
—Robert Lowell

Let me stand next to your fire.
—Jimi Hendrix

MYSTERY TRAIN

I

No Gesture: Ceremony

It goes up, engulfed in flame in seconds, until everyone
  is silent, having put,
on instruction, their cameras down, mothers boosting children
  to their shoulders,
straining for a better view. A minute or two, and the canopy
  festooning the pyre

also ignites, shrinking to ash but not falling, tumbling
  upward in the breeze,
over the crowd, and gone. Looking up to watch it flutter,
  I see how large this audience
has grown, ground awash with blankets, picnic coolers, and some,
  the program in their hands,

mouthing the printed prayers. And the body of the lama,
  within the flame,
darkening to outline. My friend tugs my sleeve
  to show me. He is deaf
and a Buddhist for ten years. He believes this lama,
  dead here in Vermont—

of, the gossip says, cirrhosis of the liver—shall be born
  again, and soon,
to Tibetan refugees in India. The dais, the pyre at its center,
  is a hundred yards away,
purple-robed monks playing cymbals and horns, genuflections and
  flourishes we can't decipher,

and around them, sealing off the inner sanctum from the public,
  the lama's private army,
clad, like British soldiers, in green berets and mufti,
  eyes fixed sternly
on the crowd. *By being here,* writes my friend on his notepad,
  we shall all be blessed.

He lives alone, an hour's drive away, a cabin without
    running water; *electricity,*
says a letter, *maybe next year.* The poems he sends me
    every month are dense,
cumbersome with puzzling imagery, and when he asks
    for advice I can offer little,

lists of books, encouragement when nothing else will help, letters
    bright with platitudes.
Write this down, he scrawls, *something must be made of this.*
    The monks stack plates
of food onto the fire, so close they must fear
    their robes will ignite,

faces and hands scalded red, and seven longbows, seven
    quivers of arrows,
symbols of his royalty, laid now on the flame. Last night,
    in the kerosene light
of my friend's kitchen table, I read from the lama's memoirs
    the badly written tale

of his flight from Tibet, hiding with his followers
    in caves from Chinese soldiers,
the struggle for months to cross the Himalayas. And my friend,
    groping for a way to put
his own life into words—abandoned, found in some apartment
    airshaft in Detroit,

almost dead from exposure, swaddled in a towel. Around him,
    torn bloody sheets
his mother never found, and then the years of foster homes,
    state schools for the deaf.
But the words, the words always failing him,
    cluttered into lies,

pages of confusion, ellipses in the oil lamp's yellow shimmer,
   and nothing I can
write to him will help, no gesture, no phrase that
   he'll read or slowly
form upon his lips. And today, as the smoke's startled odor
   filigrees into his nostrils,

he's tugging at my sleeve, waiting for his answer,
   as I wait for my own
from him. *Write this down,* he scrawls again, *something must
   be made of this.* And he's bowed
his head, put down his notepad, following the prayers, the sounds
   pentecostally strange,

low murmurs and chants all around us, gurgling up from
   his throat now, from mine.

Shroud

I could begin by telling you of nights I'd wait to hear her
    unlock the downstairs gate,
tired from dancing, her last show over and forehead
    glistening, hair
redolent of cigarettes. I could tell you she is dead now
    and not be sure of lying,

for it's been years since we last spoke. I could say that
    neither one of us exists,
because I'd have to talk instead about the click, the bob
    and wheel of the mind
as it photographs itself in the tourist-trap booth off
    Jackson Square, the magic

tawdry cabinet where the girl I was in love with then
    licked ice cream off my face,
and the flash stung our eyes. I could mention something
    tragic-sounding about
the accident, the plastic surgery, the seven months it took
    to reinvent her face.

We kept eleven Siamese cats, and I could tell you of the day
    I brought her back from
County General, no longer pretty or able to dance, though I thought
    even then I could not exist
without her. I could tell you of my husband, whom I lived with for
    a sorry alcoholic year,

how he'd ask at night, *What do women do when they do it together?*
    How could I tell him how tongue
meets tongue, how all her secret places became shrines?
    The patch would stay
another season on her eye, and it came undone as she bent
    to the cats, who circled her

quizzically, inspecting a face gone forever into its new
    unfamiliar architecture,
her body dwarflike now, cane and leather jacket, and the cats

with their quick, meteoric shivers,
turning to hide in closets, beneath the sofa. And when she began
to cry I held her head,

her stiff unreal head, and soothed her in the tones I knew
I'd have to practice getting right
for months or years if ever I would still be able
to live with her, though never
could we really touch again. There isn't much more to tell.
She called me "Ghost Dance."

I called her "Holy Shroud." Even her voice had changed,
and it swayed over me
at night, reliving every detail of its pain, the smashing
glass and metal and
the cumbersome rebirth. So it's easy to say we both
had died, easy to say

that death is a curtained booth, and you enter it
with someone you believe
you will love forever, pulling the shroud behind you,
feeding the slot its coins.
Death is someone tonguing the side of your face as the hot
hysterical light

clicks photo after photo, as she raises your skirt
while the camera watches
your face and not her hand as it kneads you and kneads you
until you begin to come,
as the camera and her hand conspire to make you close your eyes,
to open your mouth to her,

to the camera, to begin the small and frail moan
that lets death in,
so that you can't stop trembling, so that you open
your mouth still wider in
the flashbulb's dizzy glare, supplicant, beseeching,
clutching her fragrant shoulder.

9

Futures

The window gives back nothing but October fog,
    the streetlights out, the day already stalled
upon this daybed in a single room.
    Midnight bourbon, joints, and valium

let Janet sleep past six A.M. Her mother
    never spoke of nights like these, or other
nights her father's hands would halt her dreams:
    his cock, the shame, his *don't tell anyone.*

So day is shadow, the past is shame, and hate
    fills photo albums on the TV set.
Sewing machine, dress pattern, the dog-eared Keats
    her father read to her, the room a drab pastiche

of home—whatever she stuffed in the car that summer
    they died within three weeks of one another.
Bookcase, armoire, coffee creamers by the dozen
    shaped like swans. She wears the bathrobe of a lover

also dead, from Hungary, who'd drink too much
    until his English faded to a slur.
Nostalgia's unbecoming here. She'll shave
    her legs and armpits in the bath she shares

with several other "working women,"—a Renoir print,
    the makeup kits and lipsticks line the sink—
then stare all day at "futures" on a screen,
    AM EX, Dow Jones, quotations blinking green,

until she feels every day and hour as old
    as thirty-seven. Her Tarot deck foretold
that this would be her year of change:
    The Hanged Man grinning from his tree, an image

she can't shake, an image which her book suggests
    can mean *rebirth, or death, or death-
in-life.* Upside down, the blue-robed figure hangs.
    Upside down, her dazzling new lover hangs.

10

Double Exposures

99.9% are phony. It's child's play to fake a photo of a UFO.

—Carl Sagan

Ghostly over the trees, red light, blue light,
    a lava-bright glow against the evening mist,
        it must look like it's hovering in some

otherworldly physics, yet *perfection*
    means the photo is a little crude, an amateur's
        brilliant luck, Zapruder's grainy fifteen

seconds by the Book Depository, Kennedy's head
    whipped back, the "second gunman's" rifle-flash—
        the lens the needle's eye through which

someone puny enters history, his fifteen minutes
    of tabloid fame. The model is easy enough
        to rig: you ransack your stepson's *Star Wars* toys,

paint a length of drainpipe iridescent silver,
    and double A batteries power the Andromedans'
        blinking lights. Motives? Say that since

your second wife took herself and children back
    to Pittsburgh, her mother's, that every night
        you pace these rooms switching on every lamp

so you can watch the shadeless windows
    bedazzling the house as you return
        from your evening jog, the 7-Eleven, the liquor store.

Say that your days and nights have grown
    somnambulent—TV dinners, André champagne,
        porn films on the VCR, though certain

recurring dreams keep haunting you, and on
    those nights when your wife decides to phone
        it's mostly talk of money, clumsy silences

above the receiver's long-distance burr.
    All the lights are on, you hiss into
        the mirror, *but nobody's home.* And so

11

you find yourself with nylon fishing line,
    hanging the model from a ceiling hook.
        You shoot it against black drapes you've hung,

then it's superimposed against the gap
    between the elms in the vacant lot next door.
        More shots: the craft seen from several

angles. And you rehearse meticulously
    all the reporter's questions. How one night
        you wake to the blinding light, strange susurrus

of the engines. Red light, blue light,
    in the yard you click photos until you find
        you're ascending within a beam of light, the Nikon

dropping to the grass, the ground giving way until
    you're like the Chosen in some altar panel.
        Huge-headed figures beckon from

the unspeakable light inside. No mouths, no ears,
    yet it seems that they can perfectly converse
        with you, their message peace, luminous peace.

You'll look frankly at the video cam, make sure
    your eyes meet the reporter's gaze. She'll lift
        her head from her notepad, where your life

is a cuneiform of shorthand—balding, paunchy,
    unemployed, deserted by wife and children,
        hands trembling as you proclaim to all the world

their message: *Only peace. . . . They've been watching us
    for years. . . . There's still time to mend our ways. . . .
        Their spokesman now. . . . Their Emissary for this planet. . . .*

Who can tell why they've chosen me?

A Fifteenth Anniversary:
John Berryman
(January 1987)

This is not, I know, for you, though I stood on the Washington
    Avenue Bridge that day,
an acned college kid, and in the class I took from you
    all three hundred of us,
your teaching assistants not least, feared you and your wrath,
    feared the days when,

at the desk you lectured from, you'd sleep the class's
    first half hour, waking
with a start to mumble gossip on the Medicis. Two months
    and you'd be dead,
a story we all know, waving from the guardrail to passersby,
    who must have been,

at first, quite puzzled. Sometimes I'd see you
    eating breakfast alone,
Gray's Drug lunch counter, shaky and—I don't know—drunk already,
    a hand that trembled
around the egg-yolked fork. The bridge was utterly
    nondescript, the one

I aimlessly walked that day, and every day for six
    uneventful years. My students
find your poems "cranky and obscure." A dull-witted Brit
    has written your
unreadable life. I suppose you won't age gracefully, and some
    of your books, *Love & Fame*

and your gibberish sonnets, plainly are no good. But this
    is not for you:
eighteen, and dazed on Pakistani hash, I'm reading
    in a commune bedroom
The Dream Songs for the first of endless times that year.
    No Henry pyrotechnics here,

no elegy: I won't describe the moment,
    the staring, rapt,
from that February bedroom, the almost-but-not-quite-weeping,
    steaming pipe and coffee,
Muddy Waters growling from a stereo. Sunset, the neighbor below
    can't start his car,

and soon I'll dress and ride the bus to work,
    my watchman's job,
pace thirty-seven hallways until dawn, *Dream Songs* and
    a flashlight in my hand,
pages wreathed in yellow light. How wrong and petty any life is.
    This poem is not for you.

The Recent Work

He's built a large house, for himself
and his third wife, in the country,
and you're here for the dinner given to honor
the famous poet, who knows Professor B.,
the host, from college. The poet

looks drained, not just from meeting
faces he must be cordial to,
but from something deeper and more
painfully continuous, something, you think,
as American as sourceless sorrow.

Though half the guests are expatriate Spaniards,
Rumanians, all wear traces of the sickness,
as surely as the famous poet does. But isn't
"famous poet" a quaintly ironic label,
an oxymoronic delusion suffered

by college professors gifted mainly
with the knack for wishful thinking?
And yet, to imagine the famous poet
waking in a room that's
strange to him, waking to the noise of his

hotel neighbor's TV, and to imagine
the poet facing nothing more imperiling
than himself—no vial of coke,
no fifth of gin, no longing for a mistress
thirty years his junior—is to imagine

grief as bland as yours, as anyone's;
your friends who, at a restaurant table,
tell you blithely that their marriage
has gone dead. They hardly speak
to one another, haven't had sex in months.

So you think you know how the poet feels,
his finger slowly turning
ice cubes in the drink he sips from,
his knuckles white.
But you *don't* know. You drink and listen,

waiting for the first excuse
you can make to leave, but know
this will mean hours, that you'll talk
until your mouth is dry to people
you will never see again, who find you

dull as you find them, people in the "arts."
You're seated at the table now,
the poet at the head and twenty feet away;
beside you, a Spaniard whose name
you can't recall, but who says he knows you,

talking on and on about sports, his face
growing slack as he sips his wine, has more.
By now the conversation is a blur, separate
principalities of talk, the volume trebled,
and you can't help but watch the poet's face

evaporate its mask of animation,
revealing again the weary man his poems,
over decades, have tried to conceal.
And the Spaniard has finished with sports,
with gambling in Jamaica, and now

in his careful, clipped Barcelonan accent,
begins anecdotes of his years
as an officer in Franco's army, addressing
his audience of two or three. The food
is bad. Around you conversations

seem more earnest and compelling,
the poet describing, dimly, far away,
something about Robert Lowell. The voice
across from you labors on about
draftees from the provinces, children really,

illiterate, confused, who know only
that saving face means more than, as the Spaniard
puts it, "life itself." A case in point:
a draftee on the firing range, nearsighted,
nearly blind, though he's hidden this for months.

He's missing the target, repeatedly, until
your storyteller—a lieutenant then, the fifties—
removes him to the barracks. And yet
for this boy *glasses*, admitting such inadequacy,
would also mean dishonor. So that night

the boy's found dangling from a rope
tied to the barracks rafter, not
hanging long or high enough
to kill himself. They cut him down.
The man swirls the wineglass in his hand.

His name, you remember now, is Vicente.
Vicente takes the boy to the brig, where
he tries to hang himself again, and the next day
bangs his head repeatedly against the metal
toilet in his cell, hoping to finish

himself that way, though he falls unconscious
before he can do much but bleed.
Next door, the officer's lounge, Vicente—
now you're sure that is his name—
himself fears loss of face, embarrassment

before the other young lieutenants.
But how can you control a crazy man? The boy
is put in leg irons, but it will be—
and here Vicente shakes his head—
weeks before his discharge papers come.

Now—Vicente points at you—officers
are issued side arms, mainly for show.
Mine, he's telling you, had seldom
been fired, hardly ever left its holster.
But drinking next night with the other lieutenants

he calls for the boy to be
brought to the lounge, orders the guard
to remove the irons. The room's
a silent circle. Ten young officers, the guards,
all looking on. *You want so badly*

to kill yourself, he tells the boy,
then kill yourself. He hands the boy the Browning,
cocked. You can imagine, he says,
the silence. His forehead sweats
as he tells it. Traffic noise,

several watches ticking. And now the boy, trembling,
has raised the gun to his head. Vicente
mimes the gesture, his red face
melodramatically contorted. And finally
the boy squeezes the trigger.

Nothing, a click, the officers,
for a long moment, quiet,
then all of them manic with laughter.
The boy thrusts his head into
his hands, and who can tell

what's he feeling? More shame? Relief?
You can see how drunk Vicente has become.
It's late, dessert and coffee served, the poet
expressing thanks to the host. And now
the night's just epilogue. Do you

ask Vicente how he felt, picking the gun
up from the floor where the boy had hurled it,
how he feels now, telling the story?
Wiser and damned? Foolish and drunk?
Or does he tell it so often at parties

his colleagues know it almost by heart,
the gestures and pauses, the grimace
of the boy, the gun at his temple? But you
don't want to know. You must tell the poet
how much you admire his work,

the recent work especially, though you know
the critics found it self-imitation, and you,
in truth, agree with them. And it's been
a decade since his recent book,
a book you read once, years ago.

Students
(Port Townsend, Washington)

Her days mean padding through
   the bushes, whiskers a-twitch,
      smelling things, though she sees me

as shrewder and more practical
   than others see me or I see
      myself, so in my bathrobe spooning

Kal Kan in the dish we've set,
   I'm food source and she eyes me
      warily, and between bites turns

her head to keep watch for danger,
   though I'm back in the house by now, reading
      from a book on "literary theory"

how literature began when thinking
   was no longer the same
      as hearing and smelling, and writing

to a student—about metaphor—though really
   I am writing about marriage, his,
      over now, though he struggles

to resurrect it in poems, perfect it
   in lament, enlarge his song
      beyond two people who drank too much

and once threw lamps
   and scalding coffee at each other.
      He tells me he'll

grow larger now. Across the street
   she licks her paws. In the field beyond
      the street, the couple we heard

in the café last night, itinerant fiddlers,
   have lulled in sleeping bags until eleven,
      their violin cases, harbored boats,

beside them. Standing bare-assed on
the hillside, they pick up their fiddles,
look out to the water, play.

Will I ever make anything work?
Happiness writes white.
And what did you learn today?

I don't know, I don't know.
And what did you learn today?
The self is very small.

II

MYSTERY TRAIN

(A Sequence)

1.

Homage: Light from the Hall

It is Soul Brother Number One, James Brown,
Chanting, "It wouldn't be nothing, noth-iiiiinnnnnggg. . . ."
Dismembering the notes until everything hangs
On his mystical half-screech, notes skidding 'round
Your brain as you listen, rapt, thirteen,
Transistor and its single earphone tucked
With you beneath the midnight covers, station WKED,
Big Daddy Armand, The Ragin' Cajun,
"Spinning out the *bossest* platters for you all,"
Golden Age trance, when New Orleans stations
Traveling two thousand miles shaped distance
Into alchemy. Beneath the door, a light from the hall
Bathing the bedroom in its stammering glow:
Cooke and Redding risen, James Brown quaking the Apollo.

2.

Buddy Holly Watching Rebel Without a Cause, *Lubbock, Texas, 1956*

He's played hookey to see the flick again,
Though it's only showing at The Alhambra,

The run-down joint in the barrio. Spanish version,
Tawdry trashed marquee: *Rebelde Sin Causa.*

Dean staggers into Juvey, playing a credible drunk,
Though his dubbed voice squeaks like Mickey Mouse.

Me llamo Jaime Stark. But Dean's trademark smirk
Obliterates the dialogue. Buddy studies every gesture,

Hornrims sliding the bridge of his nose,
Though the smirk doesn't save that punk in the car,

Crashing to some stock-footage ocean, doesn't save Sal Mineo's
Benighted life. But Buddy, walking home, wants a *trademark.*

In shop window reflections, he practices the Jim Dean strut.
Some of us, he thinks, will never get it right.

3.

W. C. W. Watching Presley's Second Appearance on "The Ed Sullivan Show": Mercy Hospital, Newark, 1956

The tube,
      like the sonnet,
            is a fascist form.
I read they refused
      to show this kid's
            wriggling bum.
"The pure products
      of America. . . ."
            etc.
From Mississippi!
      Tupelo,
            a name like a flower
you wouldn't want
      beside you
            in a room
like this,
      where the smells hold you
            a goddamn
hostage to yourself,
      where talk's
            no longer cheap.
Missed connections,
      missed connections —
            a junk heap
blazing there in
      Ironbound,
            a couple kids
beside it,
      juiced on the
            cheapest wine. Mid-
thought. Midwinter,
      and stalled
            between the TV screen
and window. . . .
      This pomped-up kid,
            who preens
and tells us
      "Don't Be Cruel."
            Kid, forget it.
You don't know
      a fucking thing
            about cruelty yet.

4.

Matins: James Brown and His Famous Flames
Tour the South, 1958

"Please, Please, Please" on the charts permits
Four canary yellow sequined suits
And a hulking Coupe de Ville—bought on credit—
For the Alabama-Georgia roadhouse circuit.
Half last night they drove from Athens, taking turns
At the wheel. The radio hissed National Guards
In Little Rock, static filling Jackie Wilson's
"Lonely Teardrops." Parked near Macon in a soybean field,
They sleep with heads in towels to protect
Their kingly pompadours, and as the pre-dawn
Mist burns off, they wake to knocks against
The windshield. A cruiser with its siren on
Dyes the fog bright red. *Don't you niggers know your place?*
A billy club, a face, the windshield breaks.

5.

Custom Job: Hank Williams, Jr., and the Death Car, 1958

We know this story: how his daddy died of drink
On New Year's Eve, comatose in his Cadillac,
Black fins and boots splayed out the window in a grim quartet.
And in his will the car is all that's left

His son, who makes the best of it. Custom
Paint job with orange flames, chopped and channeled,
Bedazzling chrome valves and fuel injection.
Seventeen, he's cruising downtown Nashville,

Midnight, sipping sour mash from a silver flask.
He's been to see *Attack of the Teenage Werewolves*.
But there's no one out to race. He pounds time on the dash
To Carl Perkins from the radio. Neon unravels

Its Little White Way before him. Beyond it, the dark
He will cruise into, singing with it all night.

6.

Jerry Lee Lewis's Secret Marriage to Thirteen-Year-Old First Cousin Revealed During British Isles Tour, 1959. His Manager Speaks:

Dumb career move, Killer. The IRS is on your case,
Sending letters, agents. And you just say it's a *bad luck* streak?
Christ, she doesn't even menstruate!
My bookie'd give your pre-vert marriage eight weeks.
What you *talk* about at night, or need I ask?
And get this through your stupid Cracker skull:
Your little stunt's a felony in every state
But Arkansas. Get it? *Il-leg-al.*

So go ahead and play piano with your nose,
And tear your shirt off singing "High School Confidential."
But the Feds'll take the Cadillac and clothes,
Leave you without a nose to pick. They play hardball.
They'll bleed you until every penny's spent.
Your ass is grass, and where's my ten percent?

Tattoo, Corazon: Ritchie Valens, 1959

He has three singles on the charts and in
Six weeks will be dead,
          the Piper Cub that also kills

Big Bopper, Buddy Holly, and almost Dion,
Skidding to pieces in an Iowa field.

Easy to imagine premonitions—
That he wakes in night-sweats from dreams of falling—

But no.
        Harder to say he's seventeen
And buys, with cash, a house in West L.A.,

Where he's sprawled tonight, sculpting in his bedroom
A gift for his new wife. His left hand turns

The knife in circles on his right. Where thumb
And index finger meet, he cuts and squirms,

Replacing blood with ink. Cotton stops the flow.
She'll wake to heart shape,
              circling TE AMO.

8.

Fab Four Tour Deutschland: Hamburg, 1961

"Und now Ladies und Gentlemun, *Der Peedles!*"
The emcee oozes pomade, affecting the hip American,

But the accent twists the name to sound like *needles*,
Or some Teutonic baby's body function.

The bassist begins, nodding to the drummer,
Who flaunts his movie-star good looks: Pete Best,

Grinning as the drums count four. "Roll Over
Beethoven" 's the opener. McCartney's Elvis

Posturing's too shrill, the playing sloppy,
But Lennon, stoned on Romilar, doesn't care.

Mild applause, segue into "Long Tall Sally. . . ."
One will become a baby-faced billionaire,

One a film producer, one a skewed sort of martyr,
And this one, the drummer, a Liverpool butcher.

Woody Guthrie Visited by Bob Dylan: Brooklyn State Hospital, New York, 1961

He has lain here for a terrible, motionless
Decade, and talks through a system of winks
And facial twitches. The nurse props a cigarette
Between his lips, wipes his forehead. She thinks
He wants to send the kid away, but decides
To let him in—he's waited hours.
Guitar case, jean jacket. A corduroy cap slides
Down his forehead. Doesn't talk. He can't be more
Than twenty. He straps on the harmonica holder,
Tunes up, and begins his "Song to Woody,"
Trying to sound three times his age, sandpaper
Dustbowl growl, the song interminable, inept. Should he
Sing another? The eyes roll their half-hearted yes.
The nurse grits her teeth, stubs out the cigarette.

10.

The Trashmen Shaking Hands
with Hubert Humphrey at the Opening
of Apache Plaza Shopping Center,
Suburban Minneapolis, August 1963

Well-uh Bird, Bird, Bird, Bird is the Word:
The opening of their current—and what will be

Their only—hit, a ditty called "Surfin' Bird,"
Though the band was formed in Shakopee,

Minnesota, and the drummer confesses, sheepishly,
He has never seen the ocean, or even

The Great Salt Lake. Senator Humphrey
Does his balding unctuous best with them,

Stumping for next year's presidential bid.
Should Kennedy choose not to run again,

He'll be ready. And the cancer that will kill,
Slowly, and in public, this smiling public man,

Must already cruise his cells.
                            They exchange signed photographs.

"What's a Surfin' Bird?" he asks.

11.

"Mystery Train": Janis Joplin Leaves Port Arthur for Points West, 1964

Train she rides is sixteen coaches long,
   The long dark train that takes the girl away.
The silver wheels
               click and sing along

   The panhandle, the half-assed cattle towns,
All night until the misty break of day.
   Dark train,
             dark train, sixteen coaches long.

Girl's looked out her window all night long,
   Bad dreams:
             couldn't sleep her thoughts away.
The wheels click, mournful, dream along.

   Amarillo, Paradise,
             Albuquerque still a long
Night's ride. Scrub pine, cactus, fog all gray
   Around the dark train
             sixteen coaches long.

A cardboard suitcase and she's dressed all wrong.
   Got some cousin's address,
             no skills, no smarts, no money.
The wheels mock her as they click along.

A half-pint of Four Roses,
             then she hums a Woody song,
   "I Ain't Got No Home."
             The whistle brays.
The Mystery Train is sixteen coaches long.

   The whistle howls, the wheels click along.

12.

"American Bandstand" Dance Contest,
Semi-Finals, 1966

The couples bob with numbers pasted on their backs.
The girls, hair long and straight as Jeanie Shrimpton's,

Primly shake;
     the boys in cautious Beatle cuts
Jerk their heads back to show off their bangs.

This antique,
     prepsychedelic contest
Will earn the winning couple matching '66

Mustang converts, and Paul Revere and the Raiders, dressed
In powdered wigs, will play their high school dance.

Cut back to Dick Clark—
     in his arms a giant tube
Of Clearasil, the lead-in for a station break.

He peddles innocence like water from Lourdes,
And even now must keep his age a secret
       (38).

Black and white across twelve million sets
The babyface-lifted smile,
     ghostly, breaks.

13.

Delmore Schwartz at the First Performance of the Velvet Underground, New York, 1966

Lou Reed? My best student—that's the truth.
But who can stomach filthy Syracuse?
Entropy in tweed! Tenured pipe smoke
Signaling the living dead! Lou got out, chose
Tin Pan Alley over Ph.D.,
And now runs with the manic Warhol crowd.
This place: spectral Andy's Factory.
Things unravel here, the music cruelly loud,
Dissonant as mating cats. "Heroin" the song's called.
Lou sings, *it's my wife, it's my life,*
Doggerel worthy of the second grade.
Edie Sedgwick dancing, and the purple lights
Indicting everything. Lipstick fairies slither
On the dance floor. Someone's always done for.

14.

C Train Home: Lou Reed After the Wake
of Delmore Schwartz, July 1966

Strangeness woke in the motionless air. Turtleneck
Black, shades black, my best black jeans.
                                            Their heads

All turned to eye me at the open casket
Where Delmore lay propped, waxen and "beflowered,"

Grist now for some Ouija board. The 'ludes
I'd done were coming on. The room went numb:

Narcoleptic voice of Dwight McDonald
Laboring through the eulogy.
                            On the C train home,

Three greasers razz a colored maid. The little shits'
Switchblades singe the air—they just want to torment her.

No cuts, just thrills. They hop off at 35th.
We torture others or ourselves. *Delmore*—

You taught that lesson best, and lived your sullen art
To death.
            Teacher! Asshole! Here's where I get out.

15.

The Assassination of Robert Goulet
as Performed by Elvis Presley: Memphis, 1968

—"That jerk's got no heart."—E. P.

He dies vicariously on "Carol Burnett,"
Exploding to glass and tubes while singing "Camelot."

Arms outstretched, he dies Las Vegas-ed in a tux,
As the King, frenzied in his Graceland den, untucks

His .38 and pumps a bullet in the set.
(There are *three* on his wall, placed side by side.)

The room goes dark with the shot, but he gets the Boys
To change the fuses. By candlelight he toys

With his pearl-handled beauty. Lights back on,
But Goulet's vanished, replaced by downtown Saigon:

Satellite footage, the Tet offensive,
Bodies strewn along Ky's palace fences.

Above a boy whose head he's calmly blown apart,
An ARVN colonel smokes a cigarette.

16.
History Being Made:
Melcher Production Studios, Los Angeles, 1968

In the control booth, Doris Day's son,

                              Terry Melcher,
Barking commands to the engineer and drummer.

They've been here half the night—three dozen takes
Of a song entitled
                 "Beastmaster 666."

The singer mumbles through his schizy *chanson*,
Terry's latest find, one Charlie Manson,

An acid burnout stand-in for Rasputin,
Who has some trouble carrying a tune,

But Terry says he's got
                 "a certain something,
A spirit so wise and deep it's humbling,

You dig?"
               But the engineer looks skeptical,
And putters with the knobs of the control panel

As Terry speed-raps on. "Man, it's *history* being made!
In a year his name will be
                    a household word."

17.

Necromancy: The Last Days of Brian Jones, 1968

Hair fanning out, he'll float upside down,
Like the end, and beginning, of *Sunset Boulevard*.
Kicked out of the band, he's come home
To his manor in St. John's Wood—acid,

Hard drugs, delivered by minions to poolside,
Where for months on the nod he strums his National Steel,
Sprawled on a Day-Glo deck chair, lavender strobes
Festooning the water. He'll drown on his last meal,

Then fall to the chlorined deep end. But today he's dressed
As a wizard, star-checked robe and pointed cap,
Cover props from *His Satanic Majesty's Request*.
A syringe and phone are on his lap

But who does the necromancer call? Dial tone.
Hair fanning out, he'll float upside down.

18.

Photographer at Altamont:
The Morning After, 1969

A dog sleeps with a frisbee in its mouth.

A lotus-sitting girl plays the flute:

She's wearing a Confederate cap. Sleeping bag rolled out,
Her friends eat breakfast, orange juice

And jug wine. Flute joins with harmonica,
Invisible but somewhere, in a slovenly duet.
A paper bag, twisting in slow veronicas,

Plummets—*that's* the shot he wants—

Beside the flute-girl and a broken doll.
Dried blood, abstract, sinews the dirt
Before the stage,

          though he's sorry that its details,
earth tones and siennas, will be lost in his prints.
The girl lights a joint for him. He grins—

Matthew Brady posing corpses in the Devil's Den.

19.

Fragging: Armed Forces Radio, Credence on the Mekong, 1969

Brady's transistor says a Bad Moon's rising,
But here, all clouds on the unfortunate sons.
Fake stars of tracers guide the red, incoming
Fire. All night it's flared.

> *Captain Harrison's*
A dead man, growls Perez, *a fucking jigsaw*
Puzzle for the ants to eat. Any minute now
He's history. The antipersonnel's a silver claw,
The trembling pin in 'Rez's teeth. He throws

To the foxhole ahead, the captain bent there, fetal.

Grinning Brady hands white crosses to Perez,
Says the puzzle's raining down like petals
From an apple tree. The static-riddled radio blares

Proud Mary rollin' on the river.
Brady sings along,
> miming, with his rifle, a guitar.

20.

John Berryman Listening to Robert Johnson's "King of the Delta Blues," January 1972

Am I a dead man? Am I a dead man?
—Hards to say, Mr. Bones, could be.
I think some hellhound's got the scent of me.
Hear him, I do, often.
He stands like Henry's father in the black room
Filled with light. Henry's childhood home.

And Henry, like him, is undone,
Conjuring him, conjuring him.
Mad Robert Johnson did traffic with ghosts,
Which hurt themselves, coming to their lifes again.
—Why, now, Sir Bones, you messin' wif' dem?
Henry's terrible lost,

Though Henry has lived, longer by much
Than Robert Johnson, who met the devil at a crossroads,
Dead at 26.
Hellhound, truly, *do* exist.
And Henry will not sing more, either. He loads
The gin with ice cube, lemon twist.

21.
Turbulence: "Exile on Main Street" Tour, 1972

Not yet dawn, but flashbulbs pop.
                              They lurch
Across the tarmac to their private jet,

Rolling Stone logo on the tail: gaping tongue.
Mick scowls. Keith's being poured into his seat.

Pittsburgh tonight. Or is it Philly?
                              They can't
Remember which. Keith growls at his handler,

Who nods, rifles his bag for the syringe Keith wants
And sends him back to the john. He comes back
                              happier,

And with Mick goes over the playlist for tonight.
But Mick's in a nasty mood. His chardonnay's

Too warm, paté like glue, and he doesn't like
To fly in turbulence like this—makes him woozy.

The jet bucks. He bangs his fist on the windows:

"It's the *Stones* in here! The FUCKing ROLLing STONES!"

22.

Nixon Names Elvis Honorary Federal Narcotics Agent at Oval Office Ceremony, 1973

The King is thinking Tricia's got nice tits,
Of Grace Slick at Tricia's wedding, trying to spike
The punch with acid (orange sunshine, 300 hits),
While the bubblegum Turtles churned out their schlock,
And the Ehrlichmans danced the Funky Chicken.
Grace Slick named her baby *God*, a moniker,
He thinks, almost as good as *Elvis Aaron*—
Who's today shaking hands with the Chief, his mind a blur
Of dexies and reds, but scored with an M.D.'s prescription.
Pompadour, karate *ghee*, and cape,
Twenty pounds of rhinestones, a corset to tuck the paunch in:
Late model Elvis. His hands shake as he takes the plaque.
Explaining the hieroglyphic on his ring, he laughs.
"It means, sir, *Taking Care of Business with a Flash*."

23.

"It's Only Rock and Roll But I Like It":
The Fall of Saigon, 1975

The guttural stammer of the chopper blades
Raising arabesques of dust, tearing leaves
From the orange trees lining the Embassy compound:
One chopper left, and a CBS cameraman leans
From inside its door, exploiting the artful
Mayhem. Somewhere a radio blares the Stones,
"I like it, like it, yes indeed. . . ." Carts full
Of files blaze in the yard. Flak-jacketed marines
Gunpoint the crowd away. The overloaded chopper strains
And blunders from the roof. An ice-cream-suited
Saigonese drops his briefcase; both hands
Now cling to the airborne skis. The camera gets
It all: the marine leaning out the copter bay,
His fists beating time. Then the hands giving way.

24.

Malcolm McLaren Signs the Sex Pistols, London, 1976

FAUSTUS: *How comes it now that thou art out of hell?*
MEPHISTOPHILIS: *Why this is hell, nor am I out of it.*
— Marlowe

A party for them on his houseboat on the Thames.
So what they're dimwit skinheads,

              charisma-less,

Can't even play their ripped-off instruments?
He has a scheme,

          big plans for all of them.

The party gang has swarmed across the deck.
He glides among them in his shades and jewels,

Through T-shirts quilled with safety pins, tattoos
That snarl FUCK OFF,

          a python oozing down a girl's neck,

Until he spies Steve Jones and Rotten standing
Over Vicious, who is throwing up

Into a pail.
      Cute little cherub,
Ain't he? Wonderful study — heart-rending.

Wash him off.
      I've got the contracts all drawn up.
Let's go below deck, boys, where we can talk.

25.

Elvis Moving a Small Cloud:
The Desert Near Las Vegas, 1976
—*after the painting by Susan Baker*

"Stop this motherfucking Limo," says the King,
And the Caddie, halting, raises fins of dust
Into a landscape made of creosote,
Lizards, dismembered tires. The King's been reading

Again—*Mind Over Matter: Yogic Texts
On Spiritual Renewal by Doctor Krishna
Majunukta, A Guide on How to Tap the
Boundless Mental Powers of the Ancients.*

Bodyguards and hangers-on pile out.
His Highness, shades off, scans the east horizon.
"Boys, today I'm gonna show you somethin'
You can tell your grandchildren about."

He aims a finger at Nevada's only cloud.
"Lo! Behold! Now watch that fucker *move!*"

26.

Francis Ford Coppola and Anthropologist Interpreter Teaching Gartewienna Tribesmen to Sing "Light My Fire," Philippine Jungle, 1978

It's done phonetically, of course, at great
Expense. Dr. Singh, the bull-horned anthropologist,

Struts with Francis on the peopled set, insists
On short hours for the warriors, who must hunt

Wild pig tomorrow, an annual ritual
That should not be disturbed.
                              But integrity

Matters less to him than his large consulting fee.
Back in Manila, he will buy a Mercedes SL

And forget about the Leader's new doubleknits,
Leader's Number-Three-Wife
                              snorting coke with Dennis Hopper,

Brando signing glossies for the witch doctor
To grind into aphrodisiacs.
                    CAW-MAWN   BAY-BE   LIGHT

MY FOY-OR they chant.
                    "What mean *Apocalypse Now?*" asks Leader.

Dr. Singh: "Mean: *everybody-die-together-here.*"

27.

Air Guitar: Happy Hour at the Blacklight Lounge, Tucson, Arizona, 1979

Why remember that he bought the house a round,
And blundered to the stage, invisible
Guitar draped on his neck? Or black windows, never opened,
Eclipsing desert sun? *Ladies and gentle-
Men, a . . . medley of my . . . greatest hits. Doc,
Take it away. . . .* The squat Neanderthal
Behind the bar, the crowd of six, the jukebox
Shimmering on? My friend's arms Tai Chi windmills
On the stage, cheap drink hour ending to his drunken
Parodies of Jimmy Page, "Whole Lotta Love,"
Matador capework swirls, Day-Glo segue to "Jumpin'
Jack Flash"? Why remember this hooting crowd,
Black-lit yellow smiles? He bowed to them.
A few clapped hands. Six months, and he'd be dead.

—in memory of N. D.

28.
Backstage Passes:
Bob Marley's Final American Tour, 1980

His manager, a coked-up Brit, arranges
Our interview, though he adds, "Make it a quickie."
Mary totes cassette, our typed-out questions:

Do you actually regard Haile Selassie
As the Son of God?

　　　　　　　　How does ganga
Figure in your composition methods?

Explicate the politics of reggae.

But he ponders his answers, gaze intense, dread-
Locks burnished in the half-light. Bent down, pensive,
He strokes his chin.
　　　　　　　　"The music is my only message."

Then, a new exam, as if he hadn't
Taken seriously the first barrage. His face saddens,
Though the answers come in sugarcoat patois:

"You see, I will be *no* man's fool. That's all."

29.

Sandbox, Manchu Nails:
Brian Wilson in His Living Room, 1984

A fat John Foster Kane in Xanadu
It's said you've built a sandbox in your living room:

Another sixties casualty, entombed
In the Hollywood hills.
                    The Howard Hughes

Of surf and cars, you've let your fingernails
Grow long as butter knives. Your live-in shrink's

Set up for life.
                    The opulent fish tank
Of MTV, on a screen spanning half the wall,

Plays videos with the sound turned down. Slithering
Faces paddle by, as if the sea's astride your sandbox

Beach, where you're squatting now, where the pale sand sticks
To your Manchu nails, your sand castles
                              teetering.

You crawl your beach's xenophobe parameters
Of eight-by-twelve. You don't shout "surf's up" here.

53

30.

At Graceland with a Six Year Old, 1985

It's any kid's most exquisite fantasy,
To have his name
                    emblazoned on a private jet.

So Josh stares through the cockpit of
                    The Lisa Marie,
Its wings cemented to the Graceland parking lot.

The kitsch?
                    All lost on him, the gold records and cars,
Dazzling as the grave's eternal flame.

And I read him the epitaph's Gothic characters.
"A gift from God . . ." etc. Daddy Presley's wretched poem.

Colonel Parker was asked, after Elvis's death,
What he'd do now to occupy his time:
                    "Ah guess

Ah'll jus' keep awn managin' him." He's really *Dutch.*
The accent, like the colonel tag, is a ruse,

Like the living room's wall of mirrors—rigged immensity,
Pipsqueak Versailles,
                    where Josh makes faces, grinning at me.

31.

Bo Diddley at Rick's Café Americain: Long Beach Island, New Jersey, 1985

He walks forty thousand miles of barbed wire. . . . .

He wears a cobra snake for a necktie . . . . etc.

He is living, at the moment, in a Tallahassee trailer

And plays to a crowd of twenty tonight, oo-wah,
In this dive clinging to a pier, night-smell of sweat,
Excremental Jersey water. Trademark Stetson, square red
Guitar, our best homegrown surrealist:

I GOT A BRAN' NEW HOUSE ON THE RO . . . . AD . . . . SIDE
MADE OUT A' RATTLESNAKE HIDE. . . . .

                                   Between sets
He has us buy him rounds, and growls of being had,
For millions, by the record execs,
                        "all of 'em shits."

Some woman asks for "Brown-Eyed Handsome Man,"
Her favorite, she insists, of all his songs.

"That were Chuck Berry, you got the singer wrong."

32.

Roy Orbison: Comeback Tour, Tipitania's, New Orleans, 1986

Only fifty, he looks a decade older,
Jet-black shades and dye-job, and open heart
Has left a pig's vein in his left aorta.
But still, an open shirt, the twelve-inch scar,
Running from neck to navel, worn casually,
As you or I might wear our leather gloves.
A spiritless medley of his hits: "Only
The Lonely," "Blue Bayou." Of course he saves
"Oh Pretty Woman" for the encore. Then
We glimpse him shirtless, slumped backstage, a sponge
Pressed to his forehead by his latest wife, unborn
The year eight singles climbed to number one.
You mention Albert Finney in *The Dresser*,
His two hundred and twenty-seventh *Lear*.

33.

Colorizing: Turner Broadcasting Enterprises, Computer Graphics Division, Burbank, California, 1987

The process calls for twenty heads to stare
All winter at *Hard Day's Night,*
               to transfer

Color to *Can't Buy Me Love,* to Ringo
Bobbing at his BEATLES kit. And so,

With MFA in studio art (watercolor),
Lani's now employed, nonunion, by Ted Turner,

Applying "color sense" on a computer screen.
Today,
            it's John's face in the train coach scene:

She wants the flesh lifelike, a British pale,
While he croons "I Should Have Known Better," wails

Through his harmonica,
                  alive almost. Next cubicle,
Lani's friend fills in another scene, beaming Paul

Chased through alleys by his pimply fans.
She's shading his peach-fuzz,
                    the lips that form "Where's John."

34.

The Assassination of John Lennon as Depicted by the Madame Tussaud Wax Museum, Niagara Falls, Ontario, 1987

Smuggled human hair from Mexico
Falls radiant around the waxy O

Of her scream. Shades on, leather coat and pants, Yoko
On her knees—like the famous Kent State photo

Where the girl can't shriek her boyfriend alive, her arms
Windmilling Ohio sky.
                        A pump in John's chest heaves

To mimic death throes. The blood is made of latex.
His glasses: broken on the plastic sidewalk.

A scowling David Chapman, his arms outstretched,
His pistol barrel spiraling fake smoke

In a siren's red wash, completes the composition,
And somewhere background music plays "Imagine"

Before the tableau darkens. We push a button
To renew the scream.
                        The chest starts up again.

35.

Pharaoh's Palace
(Memphis, 1988)

Last week a half-crazed Mormon woman in a blue-white
    bouffant claimed
miraculous healing at the grave, hurling away her crutches
    to walk
a few unsteady feet, until a gang of courteous
    uniformed

guards restored her to her braces,
    and dispatched
her in a golf cart to the entrance. She wept in ecstacy
    or sorrow
as the iron sixteenth notes of the gate
    clattered shut.

Labor Day weekend: the day's final tour. Above us,
    the shuttered
room where the overdose took place, although
    the guards claim
heart attack. Around us in the living room,
    row upon row

of phony potted daisies, his favorite flower,
    and we walk
the arena of the dining room, its behemoth TV, the ceiling
    still patched
where the chandelier, a ton of crystal
    in the form

of a guitar, crashed last year to the table,
    a formal
setting for sixteen. In the basement snack bar
    we shudder
at the color scheme, the three TV sets side by side.
    Our guide, an incongruous patch

on her eye, tells us he "watched three stations *at once!*"
  Mirrors climb
walls and ceiling, TVs in infinite recession. Mirrors
  line the walkway
to his "Jungle Den," waterfalls cascading from
  imitation stones. The Pharaoh,

he claimed, of rock and roll. The gift shop girl
  looks up from a row
of souvenir glasses and posters. In his late-phase
  karate uniform,
rhinestones and white leather, he poses sulking
  wherever we walk.

I think of how his crooked Greek physician shot him up,
  the shut-in,
pacing his bedroom, rolling up his silk kimono
  sleeves, exclaiming
like a child when the methedrine surged in, and how
  he once dispatched

his private jet from Memphis to Las Vegas—the gleaming
  Beechcraft *Apache*—
to ferry back peanut butter and jelly sandwiches
  from some skid row
deli he remembered. But he was a *nice boy*, always,
  and claimed

his needs were simple: nymphets in white panties,
  the snow that formed
on each TV screen after "The Star-Spangled Banner" played,
  and the stations shut off
and he'd stare awhile at nothing. We weave
  down the sidewalk

to the grave, the clumsy epitaph his Daddy wrote.
　　A woman walks off
sobbing to herself. Her husband in cowboy boots,
　　face a patch
of oily sores, follows her shaking his fist, slaps her twice
　　and tells her *Godamn you, shut up.*

He drags her off by the arm, but still she's
　　wailing, sorrowfully
crouched on a bench. On the parking lot loudspeaker
　　he's performing
"Young and Beautiful." On the two-lane headed home, we stop
　　at a house claimed

by kudzu and grass, barn and house collapsed, wood a uniform
　　gray, windows shuttered.
Evening coming on: we walk a path to a family plot,
　　a hornet's nest patching
a single marker proclaiming no name, only HERE US
　　O LORD IN R SORROW.

III

Posthumous Life

London: Hampstead Heath

Jogging here, I dodge the sidewalk traffic
   of a neighborhood the Brits call "mixed,"
      Pakistani newsstands, Greek cafés, row house

gutted, row house gentrified, but then
   the still-green January heath, skyline
      beyond, the train yard where an engine pushes

freight cars to a stalled-breath halt. Here,
   the midday schoolkids, blacks on one bench,
      skinhead whites the next, duel a shrill

cacophony of ghetto blasters; machines
   scowl from their shoulders while the old ones pass,
      walking those singularly ugly mixed

breed dogs the British love. A fine rain now:
   I strain up the rise, stare off to Hampstead,
      where Keats at Wentworth Place wrote "Ode

to Autumn" in a single morning, and in
   the cottage where he worked his two
      productive years, his pen rests with a ring

made by Fanny Brawne from a lock of his hair
   brought back by Severn from Rome. Ten years older
      than Keats would ever grow, I watch a man

and woman on a bench, who cough and smile,
   incongruously spread a chessboard out,
      and as the rain intensifies, begin

to play. Middle-aged, she stares off to
   the trees beyond, stroking the odd-shaped
      chessmen as she nods and makes her move.

It's now I see the two white canes they've propped
beside them, how the chess figures are sculpted
in the bas-relief of braille,

like my grandfather's braille checkers set,
raised for black, lowered for red—on this
he taught me how to play. The woman's eyes:

cloudy blue. *Ah, Teddy,* she says to him,
superior move. Imagine their always-dark flat—
her knitting needles click as she hums

to herself, the scraping sound of his pumps
as he works his feet into them, the intricate
vocabulary of walking sounds: stocking-

foot-on-tile sound; shoe-footed sound
on carpet; the electric razor's purr
as he shaves, the noise a kind of music to her.

My grandfather, 1969, the South Dakota
nursing home: blind twenty years, the oxygen
tank for his frail, emphysemic lungs.

He asks me to shave him. The whirring razor
mingles with his stuttering breath, sour smell
against my face, a death bed scene

without Severn or the Spanish Steps,
though his posthumous life goes on
another month or two. Seventeen,

I scarcely knew him, and it was my groping
smooth-faced self I mourned as I left.
Cheap cliché of turning at the doorway,

a final look at his face, *gloom-pleased eyes
embowered from the light,* the nurse's heels
clicking toward me on the floor,

antiseptic hallway smell. How does
    forgiveness come? I have your pocket watch,
        have lost the only photograph. It's late.

The lamps click on. The rain, how fresh it must feel
    against their faces. *Teddy,* she says,
        and touches, gently, his shoulder,

I think there's someone watching us.

Azimuth

Not touching, they peer into the green and backlit
    water, where a girl, her lemon wet suit
shimmering, pets a tiny shark, who darts
    away, negotiating moonscape paths

of artificial coral. The angelfish
    and lionfish bubble into deadpan pointillist
swarms, until my father completes the canvas,
    fingers poised, white face ghosting the glass.

The Chicago Aquarium, almost
    closing time, lights breathing on and off.
My mother leans on her umbrella like a cane
    as several South Side kids, necks craned,

fidget and point at the diving girl,
    who waves, the scene a tilted spiral nebula,
kinetic and dead, light years gone. Nineteen forty-eight,
    their February honeymoon. Sunset,

Michigan Avenue silvers, as the sleet
    falls backwards, horizontal, streetlights
throbbing on. Then the long walk back to their suite
    in a nameless, indifferent hotel:

azimuth and axis mundi. Headlights
    nimbus its wallpaper, clock spitting seconds,
face a shadowy emerald. He's staring
    down the years, black mirror, the dead light whirling.

A pitcher of water on the bedside table,
    garterbelt, tie clasp, cheap string of pearls.
He sets his gin glass sweating on the dresser.
    In the bathroom's half-light, she brushes her hair.

Armageddon:
Private Gabriel Calvin Wojahn, 1900–18

PAPER DEATH SHROUD: *German, c. 1918. To conserve cloth,
and timber, then in short supply, enlisted men were
buried—usually without coffins—in such shrouds.*
            —The Imperial War Museum, London

They buried you in mud, in the standard issue
Paper shroud, like a tooth wrapped in tissue

And hidden by a child in a rain-drenched garden,
Somewhere on the Western Front, Flanders or the Somme.

No photos survive. Eighteen, illiterate,
From the family my family fled, God-mad zealots

Who beat you daily, kept all books but the Bible from your sight,
You signed your *X*, transcended to the State,

And a freight car to the trenches, the no-man's-land
Where your crazed, medieval eyes read signs,

Not words: Armageddon everywhere,
The Last Days, twitching on barbed wire.

Papists and Frenchmen served the Antichrist.
You divined the entrails of corpses, saw your fate

Augured in birds' flights, scarlet sunsets,
And one night Satan came in person to your tent,

Offering cognac, scented Parisian cigarettes,
A smoking jacket, spats, a wireless set.

You named it a *vision,* and not some dream.
You spoke of it in all the letters home

You dictated to your commandant, who'd dip your thumb
In his inkwell, press it to the thin

Blue paper. *They'll know you,* he laughed, *by your sign.*
Mustard gas killed your entire platoon.

Above the mass grave, a chaplain muttered scripture.
What survives of you? Neither words nor paper.

Garry Owen
(Port Townsend: The Bluffs)

On ten-speeds the reservists strain up the hill below,
    and the fog, florid with itself,
smokes off the tidepools. Sunlight stammering until
    we make out the vista,
concrete Rorschach blots of gun emplacements, green fatigues
    crawling barbed wire obstacles,

peering out from the mock-up of a tank. Next week they'll
    resurrect themselves
as underwriters and mechanics, but today, bandoliers glistening,
    they serve the State.
This morning downtown, we watched them yammer over
    plates of eggs and sausage,

the café olive drab with them. "It's as if," you whispered
    to me at the table,
"we lived in occupied country." The teenaged one I helped
    last night was hapless,
his nametag reading SANDERSON: 3RD CLASS. His rusty Mazda
    wouldn't start, and he wanted

to drive to town to hear the reggae band. And Sanderson,
    I remembered, was a name
on a stone we'd seen last month at Bighorn, the Custer battlefield,
    each man commemorated twice,
a stone for the spot where he fell, and a stone within
    the cemetery gates,

the site of the mass grave dug that summer by Reno's soldiers,
    the bodies maimed,
then swollen from four days in ninety-degree sun. We filled up
    in the single gas station town
of Garry Owen, named for the marching song of Custer's
    Seventh Cavalry. In 1874,

the Black Hills' expedition to survey the Sioux's most
    sacred ground—
another treaty broken—Custer brought with him a sixteen-
    piece marching band, each man
mounted on a white charger. And each morning when camp
    was broken the band would

"serenade the troops for a distance of two or three miles,
    and every night
the general would assemble the band in his tent for another
    concert." A cautionary tale:
near Mount Harney they came upon a floral valley where
    the troops could lean down

and pick flowers without dismounting, even the mule packers
    fashioning bouquets.
A concert in the field then, the band commencing "Gary Owen,"
    the horses snorting beneath crowns
of wild rose and daisy, the valley speckled blue with flung-off
    coats of picnicking soldiers.

And Corporal Sanderson, perched with his coronet
    on a granite outcrop,
recording the afternoon minutely in his notebook, which we'll see
    laid open in a glass
museum case, one hundred and ten years later, page after page
    of undecipherable description,

and, in the binding, the tiny nick where the bullet passed.
    All afternoon,
I douse you with suntan lotion, and we'll lull and drink
    like this all summer.
A single cloud leans backdrop to Whidby, Victoria Island.
    The guardsmen continue

the firing, the loading. You sit up, sip from the thermos,
    and watch through binoculars
the targets darken with holes, until suddenly you point—
    on the sound
the rising Trident sub, shark blue, lathering the water,
    a figure in a black

Sou'wester on the bridge, his own binoculars aimed back at us.

For Charles Bovary

Midnight, and your wife comes home from making
    love to a neon sculptor, nods to you
        in your chair, and tosses her beret onto
the antique phrenological head. Upstairs,

door closed, she's undressing, and soon you'll fall
    asleep with the book in your lap: Emma's
        derision of her husband after the botched
operation, the clubfoot stable boy

who'll never walk again. Another story
    whose ending you can easily predict.
        Outside, seething flakes of December snow,
two cars on the street caroming slow motion

against one another, metal on metal,
    crackling glass, and the woman from the old
        Toyota weaving to a streetlight that
she clutches, kneeling, as the college kid

crawls out from his Porsche and first inspects
    the damage to the fender. And soon you've snatched
        your bag from the closet, phoned the ambulance
and ridden the elevator to the lobby,

the street, whispering to the woman, *I'm*
    a doctor, let me see your face, does anything
        feel broken? Daubing iodine on the blue
gash on her cheek you tell her no, you don't

think it will scar very badly, though you're thinking
    how the noise must have troubled your wife's
        surely erotic dreams—the sculptor in his loft
undressing her beneath the green and orange

neon beer signs, how in the dream he must
    be someone other than the man you met
        last summer at the opening. The dream hands
that peel her bra and jeans off must be gentle,

not paint stained, don't reek of oil, and you want
    it to end just before he enters her,
        want the crash to have wakened her so she stares
perplexed about the bedroom, relieved

to know you're not asleep beside her. And now
    the woman's weeping so relentlessly
        against your shoulder that you can't make out
what she's saying, while the college kid sways shivering

against the brownstone's iron fence beyond.
    Before the ambulance arrives you know
        you'll close the wound and try to calm her with
the words you can't, after all these years, get right,

know again the story's finish: you're
    the one who outlives them all, the only one
        who'd let himself believe he could die
a martyr to love, awkward and stupid

in the snow, truly shameless to the end.

Signs and Wonders

Famous paintings duplicated on the sugar packets—sunflowers
    at Arles, *The Damsels of Avignon,*
miniscule *Blue Boy.* The waitress pours more coffee. He's staring
    out the truck stop window
at the phone booth where his wife, shrouded in scarves and his
    down jacket, is talking

long distance to the man she plans to leave him for. She gestures
    beside the receiver,
her things already packed in the car, an hour more to Boston,
    and the snow not letting up,
the airport closed. *Impression: Rising Sun. Clothed Maja.*
    Naked Maja. Nighthawks,

of course, *at the Diner.* The hollow thought, as his wife
    once told him,
that imagination and memory are one. He stuffs the packets
    in his shirt pocket,
already living an evening months or years ahead,
    when he'll drink too much, remove

the packets from a drawer, turn them over again, again, a rapt
    night of signs and wonders.
And what beyond this? The snow falling harder. His memory
    of a story she once told him—
how as a child she stuttered, horribly. What year was it?
    Fourth grade? Fifth?

That morning, the class had been shown an ancient documentary
    film of Helen Keller,
in which, in the only scene his wife could remember, Helen
    Keller places her hands
very gently—*elegantly,* his wife said—on the neck of Benny Goodman,
    so that her fingers can "hear,"

through his trembling vocal cords, a Bach fugue, some Gershwin.
   Is this how she recalled it?
Later, the teacher made her stand before the classroom
   to read, until it was
recited impeccably, a book report. And how long it took,
   each syllable

a heavy weight to lift. From fear, from the shame, she had
   wet her pants before everyone,
and could not return to school for weeks. And yet,
   as she told the story,
she added that she sometimes wished she could have
   the stutter back,

how the hissing, awkward stammer would protect her
   from the world,
a world where tonight the snow has careened its way
   from Canada, the North
Dakota plains, across Pennsylvania, to *this* place, *this* time,
   where he watches her

talk on and on, but knows that neither one of them
   is really here,
and she's murmuring to a voice emerging from the snow,
   then turning toward
the café's pink, seething neon, turning toward
   her husband's face,

disembodied, flickering in the window's square of light.

Diary Pages: Amsterdam
No. 263 Prinsengracht, 1979

Anne Frank bore no adult grief, but what is adult grief?
    The day your lover left
you climbed with her and thirty Belgian schoolkids up
    the stairway to the secret
passageway, the famous bookcase door, the hushed
    surreptitious rooms

of three years' hiding: the diary pages, whispered meals
    of turnips, and her desk
in a corner, her wall still collaged with peeling movie stars,
    Robert Taylor's Ivanhoe,
Marlene Dietrich in male drag—cigarette holder,
    top hat askew. Then,

the hallway of requisite statistics, flanked with photo blow-ups,
    JUDEN and a dripping
swastika beside the broken windows of a shop. And farther on,
    heaped Treblinka corpses,
the Warsaw ghetto dead. The Belgian teacher tried to shield
    her uniformed boys and girls.

But the ones who stole a look seemed not to care, and the rest
    were busy with the bookcase door,
the detail they'd remember best. Your fiancée laughed
    along with them in French, put you
inside the room and shut the door, to demonstrate. You were both
    fucked-up on the hash

you'd smoked downtown, the *yongen ginever* you'd ordered to toast
    her departure. And now
the long walk back to the central station, rain-pocked canals
    laid out in grids like Mondrians,
red-light district windows where the whores displayed themselves,
    animated mannequins,

running tongues along the tinted panes. But the station scene—
    whatever words you spoke,
they're not recorded. You both knew that soon you'd break it off,
    a few blue-papered letters
from her school in the south of France. You were going that fall
    to a job back home,

and returning that night to the coldwater B & B
    the two of you had shared,
you turned the fetish of the purple woolen glove she'd
    accidentally left
over and over in your hands. You drank yourself sick. Why, today,
    must you read this again?

Behind the bookcase door, no place for the error that you called
    our grief, our pity. Miniscule,
languid sorrows—what did you know of anything?
    Marlene Dietrich,
top hat tipped in benediction for a girl, an ordinary girl,
    whose heights, as she grew,

are still marked in pencil on a door frame, whose small map—
    with pushpins—charted
the Allied advance. A glass case: your hands ran over the wavering
    borderlines. Hubris to say
she'd want a life like yours that day, want such amplitude
    of self-regard. But what else,
if you even could, would you give to her? Lucky bastard:
    she could never be like you.

In Hiding

After Franco's victory, Manuel Cortes, socialist and soldier of the
Republic, spent thirty years in hiding in the attic of his home.

From the attic's shutter crack I watch
Juliana recede down the road to Malaga,
    her egg baskets aglow in dawnlight,
and I turn from yesterday's papers, the radio

humming low so the neighbors won't hear:
Franco guiding Eisenhower through
    the NATO base at Torrejón, a marching band,
the B-47s grumbling as they rise

laden with napalm and atom bombs, the way,
in '37, the Nazi Heinkels rumbled over Guernica,
    our battalion, the 101st, peering up
from the trenches as the bombs surged down,

and if not for the noise it looked
like a man shelling peanuts on a sidewalk,
    innocent litter that pigeons would eat
on a sun-drenched day in the spring, when you smell,

as you can today, the lemon blossoms—but yellow smoke
laddered the sky, and the faces
    of the dying in Cathedral San Xavier
we could only imagine, like images

remembered from a film seen years
before. So much one can only *imagine:*
    this attic room unchanged for decades,
and Conchita now with a child of her own,

and Juliana tells me all along
the road from Torremolinos to Malaga
    the villas of the rich, Americans
and Madrillino doctors, gaze out

on the sea, Hollywood men, their women
precious stones, sunning themselves

79

each afternoon on the balconies.

❊

But isn't this also a life of leisure?
   I weave, some mornings, mats of esparto grass
      Juliana will sell in the city,
and some nights try to read again

the difficult chapters of *Kapital.*
   Even those mornings when De Valente's
      Guardia Civil, all of them drunk,
would ransack Juliana's wardrobe, tear

her slips and nightgowns from the dresser
   to find some evidence of me,
      my waiting here, only this wall
between me and the firing squad—was leisure.

I counted time, like a blind accordionist
   tapping his boot to the music,
      his ears by now so acute
he still can hear his heartbeat

among the loud notes of his reel.
   Time, it comes down to, and timing.
      As mayor, as soldier, I believed in
The People, in bread for them, and land.

To believe in them now, I believe
   in this waiting, asking to keep
      the waiting holy, uncompromised by memory,
though some nights I'm still faltering

knee-deep through snow in Catalonia,
   my boots turned rags, the wound
      in my neck, where the bullet passed,
stanched with a scarf, my comrade

80

a Jewish corporal from Mérida,
      moaning for his sweetheart on my back,
         the dark hole in his chest
all night dampening my shoulder.

✿

      Last year Conchita, my only child,
married the village postal clerk,
a man who does not know I exist. With my
         smuggled champagne I stared through the shutters

      at the wedding dance in the courtyard below,
and wept, not for her, but for my own absence,
the way a ghost must weep, continually,
         for things it lived with and touched.

      But later, I found myself humming
to the band as it yelped its tunes,
yet softly, so no one would hear.
         Then the guests were home, yellow lights

      still strung in the olives. The musicians,
ties and jackets draped on wicker chairs,
wiped sweat from their brows and gently placed
         in their cases the heavy accordions.

      Always people say you walk
ahead into the future, though in truth
you walk backwards toward it, and only
         the past spreads its vista before you,

      though always, my friends, it is fading.
And you try to remember what it is that you
believed in. You try very hard.
         You wait. You watch until it's gone.

The Resurrection of the Dead:
Port Glasgow, 1950

A painting by Sir Stanley Spencer, Tate Gallery

Gingerly they rub their eyes against
    the sunbeams' innumerable golds,
        harmless swords in some magician's trunk.

They don't all wake at once. This couple: the wife's
    kiss startling her husband to life, her shroud
        a kind of negligee she fidgets with,

suddenly shy, while her man dusts off his bowler hat,
    and taps his pocket watch alive again.
        Groups have swarmed around the background's

shanty town of crypts, struggling with crowbars
    at the sealed doors. From inside, arms snaking out.
        The dizzying profusion of rebirth,

and everyone has grown mysteriously
    plump in death! Cherubs in tweed, fugitive *putti*
        from some Mannerist chapel ceiling. Yet surely

the effect's heroic. They storm the mausoleums
    like some Eisenstein montage, the winter
        palace fallen, and it's summer: everywhere

a dazzle of larkspur, splayed narcissi,
    and now it shall be summer for eternity.
        I believed that the summer of 1980

would last forever. I shuffled food trays
    in a Tucson hospital, the hottest and driest
        months on record. And because I'd been to college

I was spared the mopping and bedpan details, and instead
    read magazines and Sidney Sheldon paperbacks
        to patients who could not read for themselves:

stroke-blind Edna, a cataract case named Mae,
    and on the burn ward, for an hour each
        afternoon, it was Batman comics for a boy

named Carlos—his family illegals from Mazatlan—
   whose father, drunk, had hurled a pan of scalding
      cooking oil on his face and shoulders,

broken two of his ribs and an arm, though Carlos
   could not recall what he'd been punished for,
      and had languished on the ward for seven months.

The skin grafts—the flesh so delicately pried
   from his stomach and thighs, and woven gracelessly
      into his face and neck—refused to "take."

The face would not allow itself rebirth.
   The dressings on his head and shoulders made him look,
      he'd say, like Batman, the Cowled Crusader.

I'd explained the odd English words to him, COWL-ED
   and CRU-SAD-ER slithering off my tongue.
      He liked the sound. *Open the cowl of the window,*

he'd tell me, *and let me see the sun.* Or,
   It hurts me, under my cowl today. Who knows
      what became of him. Nineteen-eighty's summer ended

with a job back East, and money enough to pack
   my things into a rusty Nova, bolt
      from my lease, and drive. And Carlos, I suppose,

remained the Cowled Crusader of his endless
   burn ward summer. Someone else would read to him,
      and probably, in time, a foster family

would be found, who couldn't help but cringe
   in secret at the doctors' botched salvation
      of his face—as he poured his breakfast milk, or huddled

in some chair to watch cartoons. *Behold*
   how the dead have risen, giddy and uncorrupted
      into the transfiguring summer light.

83

They rise into a world so huge it spans
    an enormous gallery wall. Moon-faced, grinning immortals,
      what can you say to him, a man by now,

as he stares into each morning's mirror and lathers
    the pale half of his face that he can shave?
      What do you say as he covers the wounded side,

rubs the steam-fringed mirror and curses,
    softly, to himself in Spanish?
      I want you to move closer. Feel

his breath on the napes of your living necks.
    Stroke, if you can, his face. You—the risen,
      the born again—how can you turn away?

Notes

The poems of section 2 are sometimes based on apocryphal or wholly invented incidents. Most, however, were inspired by various histories and biographies, too numerous to name. And, of course, several decades of rock and roll music.

The italicized passages in lines 55 and 56 of "Posthumous Life" are from Keats's "Sleep and Poetry." "Garry Owen" draws upon material from Evans Connell's *Son of the Morning Star* (North Point, 1985). "In Hiding" was inspired by an oral history of the same title compiled by Ronald Fraser (Pantheon 1971), based on interviews with both Manuel and Juliana Cortes.

"The Resurrection of the Dead, Port Glasgow, 1950": Spencer painted two large resurrection scenes, "The Resurrection: Cookham-on-Thames" (1929, also in the Tate), and the subject of my poem, one of his last paintings.

"No Gesture: Ceremony" is for Tony Whedon; "The Resurrection of the Dead" for Mark Doty. Finally, my gratitude to those friends whose advice and support helped me to complete this collection: Jim Harms, Dave Jauss, Richard Lyons, Bill Olsen, and Dean Young.

About the Author

David Wojahn was born in St. Paul, Minnesota, in 1953, and was educated at the University of Minnesota and the University of Arizona. His first collection, *Icehouse Lights,* was selected by Richard Hugo as the 1981 winner of the Yale Series of Younger Poets competition, and was also chosen as the Poetry Society of America's William Carlos Williams Book Award. His second collection, *Glassworks,* was published by the University of Pittsburgh Press in 1987, and was awarded the Society of Midland Authors' Award for best volume of poetry published during that year. He has received fellowships from the National Endowment for the Arts, the Fine Arts Work Center in Provincetown, and in 1987-88 was the Amy Lowell Traveling Poetry Scholar. He has taught at the University of New Orleans, the University of Arkansas at Little Rock, and the University of Houston. He presently teaches at Indiana University, where he is Lilly Associate Professor of Poetry, and in the MFA in Writing Program of Vermont College.

PITT POETRY SERIES

Ed Ochester, General Editor